IMAGES
of Scotland

ABERDEEN

THE BEACH AND BATHING STATION ABERDEEN.

—TO ABERDEEN.

I have had so much on my shoulders since I've been at Aberdeen, that I get no chance to write letters, so post cards must do.

Long before package holidays abroad were conceived, a day at the seaside was considered a perfect way to spend some leisure time. The railway had reached Aberdeen in 1850 and the city was quickly to become a popular holiday resort. A visit to the beach was a perfect opportunity to send someone a postcard; how could anyone disagree with the sentiment of this 1908 postcard?

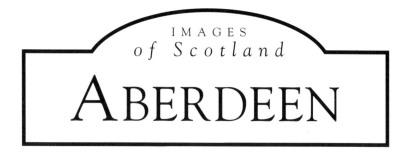

IMAGES
of Scotland

ABERDEEN

Compiled by
Alistair Burnett

TEMPUS

First published 1999
Copyright © Alistair Burnett, 1999

Tempus Publishing Limited
The Mill, Brimscombe Port,
Stroud, Gloucestershire, GL5 2QG

ISBN 0 7524 1828 9

Typesetting and origination by
Tempus Publishing Limited
Printed in Great Britain by
Midway Clark Printing, Wiltshire

For these youngsters from Torry, a dip in the River Dee was their perfect day. The early days of the twentieth century must have been an age of innocence; would this photograph be considered a mite inappropriate today?

Contents

Acknowledgements

I would like to thank all those whom, knowingly or unknowingly, have helped in the compilation of this book. The bulk of the material contained in this book forms part of my postcard collection gathered over a number of years. To all those postcard publishers, many from a bygone era, may I express a sense of obligation; each postcard helps to provide a permanent record of our local history.

Any errors contained in the book are totally my responsibility, but I would claim them as unintentional and hopefully of a minor nature. An appreciation of old photographs and nostalgia will be offered in my defense. I also find it important to acknowledge any original copyrights.

Finally, special thanks to Eleanor, Lucy and Albert, who have each, helped me in their own particular manner. Their support has been priceless.

Introduction

The growth and development of Aberdeen reflect those of other major cities, but its changes have been more striking than many. Hopefully this book will illustrate such changes, changes that have not always been met with universal approval. Change does come on its own, but perhaps that is only nostalgia speaking.

Aberdeen in the early nineteenth century was a prosperous booming city. The population by 1840 had reached 63,000 with some twelve thousand people employed in the predominant textile industry, exporting linen and woolen goods to Europe. The construction of major thoroughfares began in earnest: Union Street and Union Bridge (1805), King Street (1804), Great South Road (1807) and George Street extended to North Broadford (1805). Rapid expansion of streets from the newly completed Union Street and Union Bridge continued unabated from the 1820s until in 1890 the Town Council controversially renamed the upper or west end part of Union Street, then known as Union Place, to merge the whole line of street into one street. This decision appalled local residents.

Throughout the nineteenth century, the granite industry flourished as local architects Archibald Simpson and John Smith favoured the abundance of local stone to build the world renowned 'Granite City'. Besides local demand for granite, its export potential was soon realised with over 70,000 tons annually exported by 1898 to mainly the United States. Popular with Queen Victoria and Prince Albert, they commissioned John Smith's son, William, to design and build the new Balmoral Castle. This new fashionable material was employing 2,700 people at its peak and became synonymous with the city of Aberdeen as well as paving the streets of London 'with gold.'

The impact of railways and radical improvements in the harbour area exploited the potential of Aberdeen as a major fishing port. The diversion of the River Dee in 1871 to 1873, and the construction of new fish markets and tidal dock to accommodate steam trawlers, led Aberdeen to quickly becoming the leading trawler port in Scotland. The new railway system of 1850 allowed fresh fish to be transported south to the English market.

By the late nineteenth century more changes were to affect Aberdeen. The city extended its boundaries in 1891 to include Woodside, Old Aberdeen and Torry; the latter now connected by the Victoria Bridge (1881). The city deservedly exuberated its confidence with schemes to provide Aberdonians with the facilities of a modern city. Schools, public parks, hospitals, sewage works, gas and electricity, were all improvements inaugurated for the benefit of a population now reaching 150,000. Civic structures included a trio of buildings at the end of Union Terrace – 'Education, Salvation, Damnation,' representing a library, a church and a theatre. However, the building that best signified the prominence of the city was Marischal College. Major extension work was completed in 1906, making it the world's second largest granite structure.

In the period after the First World War, some industries initially flourished. The year 1925 saw a record 130,000 tons of fish landed, and fishing remained a fundamental part of the local economy well into the 1950s. The granite industry, however, never reached the peaks of the pre-war years and the textile industry was virtually decimated, with only Richards at Broadford and Crombie at Grandholm surviving, but employing significantly reduced numbers. The relative decline of the 'old staples' saw local Aberdonians suffering unemployment and even poverty during these years of depression. The picture was not all doom and gloom in these inter-war years, with an extensive house building program undertaken that replaced slums with tenements to relieve overcrowding. Private suburban housing spread towards King's Gate and only the outbreak of the Second World War curtailed the increase of bungalows. Progression was also illustrated with the development of new housing estates, better bus services and more private cars. However, in keeping with the generally less assured times, there was a return to plain, even austere civic buildings. The Bon Accord Baths and Rosemount Square became the last of the granite monuments of Aberdeen as the cost became too great.

The priority in the 1950s was a need for large numbers of council houses and with land at a premium the invariable happened. The next decade was the birth of the multi-storey tower blocks, starting with green field sites at Ashgrove, Hazlehead and then on to redeveloping the central areas of Skene Street, Gallowgate, Castlehill and Hutcheon Street. This desire for modern blocks was not limited only to housing but also to public and civil buildings. Few would argue that the city had improved its architectural grace. Norco House (1966), the building Aberdonians love to hate, was built by the Northern Co-operative Society as an example of a modern department store. In 1987 these premises were taken over by the John Lewis Partnership. The demolition of Archibald Simpson's New Market building in Market Street, in 1971, to be replaced by a shopping centre, galvanized an increase in conservation pressure groups and a realisation that change may not necessarily mean total destruction.

The North Sea oil boom of the 1970s and 1980s was the most radical change to have ever happened to Aberdeen. It created over 40,000 jobs, with unemployment rates less than half the national average. It led to soaring house prices and pressures on the industries to find both suitable commercial and residential properties for the influx of services and people attracted to the city. Those in employment and earning good wages need a means of spending and developers and entrepreneurs were able and willing to provide such amenities.

The Aberdeen of today is a prosperous, vibrant city and an extraordinary place to live and bring up a family. You can visit the Queen's Link Pleasure Park with entertainment for all ages, whatever the weather or time of day, or spend to your hearts content in the Bon-Accord Centre with over forty-six shops and three major stores to tempt you. If you want a meal or a drink, the list is endless. Aberdeen, like nostalgia, is not like what it used to be, but there are few cities better prepared for the arrival of the twenty-first century.

One

At Your Leisure

The original Winter Gardens at the Duthie Park were constructed in 1900 from timber and glass and heated by hot water pipes, all at a cost of £1,550. Following storm damage in 1969, the building was demolished. The new Winter Gardens are the largest in Europe.

3790 In Duthie Park, Aberdeen.

Sailing a yacht in the pond at the Duthie Park, as this scene from 1930 would suggest, was clearly a serious business and not only as a pastime for children. The small boy in the front of the picture is holding a yacht in his hand, but must feel somewhat overshadowed by the competition.

DUTHIE PARK, ABERDEEN. (9)

A group of children are waiting eagerly for their trip on the paddleboats at the Duthie Park. The boats were propelled by hand and it was possible to go fairly fast as long as you had the strength to keep going. To help lengthen the sailing time it was a good idea for your paddleboat to be at the opposite end of the pond when your boat number was called.

Duthie Park was gifted to the city by Miss Elizabeth Crombie Duthie in 1883 as a memorial to her brother and uncle and has continued to be an attraction to generations of Aberdonians. Three Edwardian children are seen posed in front of the McGrigor Obelisk, a memorial to Sir James McGrigor, Director General of the Army Medical Department and Lord Rector of Marischal College. The obelisk originally stood in the quadrangle of Marischal College but was removed to its present spot after the extensions to the college in 1906.

A splendid day down at the beach sometime in the 1920s. The bathing station, designed by the city architect John Rust, was opened in 1895, and in its day was the height of sophistication. It could boast a swimming pool and a section for private baths. Better known as the Beach Baths, it was, until its demolition in 1972, always to be remembered for the cold changing rooms and the smell of chlorine.

The beach is crowded, so one must assume that the picture was taken sometime in the summer, yet everyone is dressed in heavy outdoor clothes. Back in the 1920s it was the custom to sit on the sand with your normal, everyday clothes. Beachwear had yet to be thought of unless you were actually going for a dip in the sea. Having said that, it does seem a trifle formal to be standing on the beach in a suit, and wing collar and tie with a walking cane.

It is not surprising that in 1926 Thomas Roberts and Hume won an architectural competition for their design of the Beach Ballroom, perfectly typifying the era. This picture evokes memories of nights spent dancing the evening away before stepping into the cold and heading home. The only thing wrong with the Beach Ballroom is that it is in the wrong place!

Even in 1927, the beach promenade was the place to be seen and to show off the latest fashions. How long did it take the photographer to spot these two belles?

469   The Promenade, Aberdeen Beach

The beach has always been a magnet for a family day out and what could be more fun than a ride on a pony? The name Duckworths can be seen above one of the amusements. Henry Duckworth was a showman who first brought the scenic railway to Aberdeen, an idea he imported from the USA.

13

In 1910 there was no leisure centre to amuse the crowds who flocked to the beach, but look at what was on offer. This proud young man was the first winner at the 'children's day at the beach.' One can only wonder what he won.

Another scene from the same day and look at the spectators. Have you ever seen so many people wearing hats? The sack race was so popular that a policeman was required to keep the crowds in check! Note in the background the Electric Picture House. Who needs a leisure centre?

The main attraction at the pleasure beach in the 1930s was the scenic railway. There was even a conductor on board to safeguard the passengers. The railway met a sad ending when it was badly damaged in a fire in 1940; but those are the ups and downs of showbiz!

A stroll along the promenade has always been a popular pastime where you could stop and buy an ice cream. Rows of bathing machines face the water. By 1930, when this photograph was taken, the practice of towing the huts down into the sea using donkeys to preserve the bather's modesty had stopped.

A similar view but thirty years on and the ice cream kiosk is now owned by P. Vicca, a name synonymous with the beach promenade.

The Links has always been a popular play area for all ages. Golf has been played on the Links since 1625. The children's play facilities were laid out to recreate a fishing village, with a harbour, boats, nets and even a railway station. In the background a cricket match is in progress and the floodlights of Pittodrie Football Ground are barely in view.

Hazlehead Gardens belonged to the Rose family until 1920, when the city acquired the land and began the development of the golf courses and the park. The history of Hazlehead can be traced back to the days of Robert the Bruce and was part of the Forest of Stocket, gifted to the Aberdonians in 1313 for services rendered to the King.

THE CAFE, HAZLEHEAD, ABERDEEN.

The Rose family, who were wealthy ship owners, had built a mansion in Hazlehead in 1775. The house was put to use as a cafe by the Town Council and is an appropriate background to this nostalgic view of an outing in the park in the late 1920s.

In 1958 the old mansion was replaced by this rather ordinary looking building. Judging by the crowds in this 1960 scene, the new venture must have been a roaring success and there is a huge queue of people waiting to buy refreshments. It would have been hard work for the staff who had to work in the tearooms in the height of the summer.

Hazlehead Park, Aberdeen   33616

No, these are not wild beasts roaming the grounds of Hazlehead; these animals were conveniently positioned around the grounds and were perfect props for photographs. There must be few children who visited Hazlehead Park in the 1950s and 1960s who did not end up in a photograph next to a wild beast!

The city acquired Westburn House and grounds in 1899. The house was built in 1845 for David Chalmers, a grandson of the founder of the *Aberdeen Journal*, and was the work of Archibald Simpson. The house, partly obscured in this picture, has recently fallen into disrepair. The statue in the front of the picture is in fact a drinking well, presented to the citizens of Aberdeen by The Good Templars in 1876, in honour of the introduction of their order into the district in 1870. This photograph was taken around 1910.

4012   THE POND, WESTBURN PARK, ABERDEEN

Westburn Park is perhaps better known today as the venue for the Lawn Bowl World Championships, but as this 1940s picture illustrates, children and paddling pools are a natural combination. This scene could be recreated any sunny day ever since the park was created in 1901. The stream that flows through the park was once known as the Clerkseat Burn.

A truly delightful picture, taken at the turn of the century, of a group of children playing in front of the fountain in Victoria Park. You would have to be big and strong to push that size of perambulator. Victoria Park is the city's oldest park, established in 1871.

A game of draughts in Union Terrace Gardens was a serious business, as this 1950s scene demonstrates, and clearly a popular spectator sport. Could there be an argument for including outdoor draughts at a future Olympic Games?

Opposite: Union Terrace Gardens were laid out in 1891-1893 by John Morgan, Aberdeen's most prominent builder, and openly attract comparison with Edinburgh's Princess Street Gardens. This 1956 scene could easily be an advert for the Tourist Board with highland dancers performing in the park, overlooked by His Majesty's Theatre, glistening in the sunlight.

A band playing in Union Terrace was an event guaranteed to attract a large crowd and for many an opportunity to relax and enjoy the music. Harry Gordon, the Laird of Inversnecky and Aberdeen's finest comedian, was making his first appearance at His Majesty's Theatre when this photograph was taken in 1923.

The Bon Accord Baths, which opened in 1940 and could be best described as akin to a granite box. Designed by the city architect Alexander McRobbie, it is better known to Aberdonians as the 'Uptown Baths.' This busy scene from the 1950s underlines that the rather austere exterior was complimented by an impressive art-deco interior. A perfect end to a session spent swimming had to be a visit to the chip shop.

Two
Walkin' the Mat

It is difficult to believe that the tram car stop was actually in the middle of Holburn Junction, but the pedestrians from this 1910 scene seem unconcerned. Bicycles, horses and carts, would suggest Union Street was more relaxed than perhaps it is today. The view from the top of the tram must have been worth the fare alone.

HOLBURN JUNCTION ("BABBIE LAW") ABERDEEN

Another view of Holburn Junction almost thirty years later, and road safety has become more relevant; note the 'Belisha Beacons' and the tram stop now on the pavement. Holburn Junction was sometimes known as 'Babbie Law,' named after the proprietor of a shop near the junction where the carters, loaded with granite from Rubislaw Quarry, would stop for a drink on their way to the granite yards.

HOLBURN JUNCTION AND ALFORD PLACE, ABERDEEN   D 5471

A rather dated picture from the 1960s, but note on the left, the often-overlooked landmark of the United Free Church College, built in 1850 to train ministers. Today, it is used by the University of Aberdeen. Alford Place was originally called Alford Road but that was in the days when it was a rough country road leading west to Upper Donside.

The West End of Union Street was better known as Union Place until 1890 and was predominantly residential. Characteristic features of the houses were the railings and steps leading to the front door. As Union Street became more commercial these features gradually disappeared.

The Capitol Picture House opened in 1933 and was the jewel in the Donald Cinema Empire. At the peak of its popularity, there were nineteen cinemas in Aberdeen and in pre-television days a visit to the pictures was the night out for most people. Those were the days when the cinema presented two feature films at each performance and at the end of the evening 'God Save the King' was played and everyone stood to attention.

Tramway tracks still dominated Union Street in the 1950s, but the days of the trams were finally numbered on 3 May 1958. The final journey was between the Bridge of Dee and the Bridge of Don. To help celebrate this milestone the whole tram fleet was burned at the beach terminus later that month. The tram has since made a comeback, although not in Aberdeen, with both Sheffield and Manchester having reintroduced the system to their cities.

Note the 'Sold' sign on the building on the right, considered by many to be one of the most handsome town houses in Aberdeen. It was built in 1810 by John Smith for a Peter Milne of Crimonmogate. Later it became the premises of the Royal Northern Club but was demolished in 1963 and replaced by a modern shopping block.

The Assembly Rooms were built in 1822, originally as a town club, to entertain wealthy landowners. It is regarded as the most outstanding building on the whole of Union Street – the style is neo-Grecian and was designed by Archibald Simpson. The Concert Hall was added in 1859 and this elegant building has become better known as the Music Hall. It is frightening to think that in the early 1960s there was a proposal for it to be demolished.

A typical 1930s scene and a policeman in a white coat is given the task of directing the ever-increasing traffic. Seated around King Edward VII's statue is a group of elderly men, all wearing bonnets and watching the world go by.

UNION BRIDGE AND TRINITY HALL, ABERDEEN (26)

The imposing Tudor style building in this view from the early 1950s is Trinity Hall, built in 1846 for the Seven Incorporated Trades (Hammermen, Tailors, Fleshers, Cordwainers, Baxters, Weavers and Wrights, and Coopers). It was better known as McMillan's and could boast the best toy department in town. In 1963 a shopping development culminated in the widening of Union Bridge and the reduction for McMillan's.

In front of the Palace Hotel, a street sweeper can be seen cleaning up after the many horse-drawn vehicles. The Palace Hotel was built in 1873 and was owned by the Great North of Scotland Railway Company. The Joint Station in Guild Street was accessed by a private lift into the hotel. Following an air raid in October 1941, the hotel was burned down in a dramatic blaze that claimed six lives. Since then the site became the home of C&A's, who later moved to the Bon Accord Centre.

Union Street in 1901 and look at the hub of activity on the bridge; bicycles, handcarts, horse and carts and to the far west, a lone tramcar is the only mechanical vehicle to be seen. The bridge is flanked by the Palace Hotel and the Northern Assurance Company's building to the right, sometimes known as the Monkey House and used as a meeting place by generations of Aberdonians.

A characteristic 1960s scene with Union Street dominated by buses, the tramlines having been lifted in 1958. To the left is the Queens Cinema, closed in 1981. This handsome building began life as a meeting place for advocates in 1837, but was later altered to become the Queen's Rooms restaurant.

The corner of Union Street and Back Wynd is a perfect setting to admire the spire of St Nicholas church. Known as the Mither Kirk, it has been in existence since at least 1151. A fire in 1874 destroyed the spire and part of the Kirk but William Smith rebuilt it in 1877. In 1905, when this photograph was taken, afternoon tea rather than a film was on the menu at the Queens'.

Cabbies wait for business in front of one of the most impressive features of Union Street. John Smith's Facade was built in 1829, to front the St Nicholas' churchyard. The cemetery is the resting place of many of the city's prominent families, but before being extended in 1819 the land was used by travelling shows and circuses. Open-topped trams date this scene from before 1904.

A scene from the mid-1920s and the mode of transport has moved on. Single-deck buses were first introduced to the City in 1920 and thanks to the technological advantages gained from the Great War; motor buses were now considered an option to the tramcar. Tramcar No. 103, seen heading away from the camera, was introduced into the fleet in 1925 and was still in operation on the last day of the tram service in 1958.

Queen Victoria watches over this bustling scene around 1900, a view that has all but disappeared. Samuel the jewellers was replaced by the Commercial Bank in 1936, while the great road north out along George Street is no longer accessible except to pedestrians willing to weave their way through two extensive shopping centres. The Queen herself flitted to Queen's Cross in 1964. The Woodside tramline closed in 1955.

This late 1930s view of Union Street features the newly built Commercial Bank of Scotland by Jenkins and Marr, probably the last classical building to grace Union Street. On the opposite corner you can see Falconers, later to be taken over by Frasers. This was a good example of how a modern department store could take over an existing set of buildings and still maintain the original character.

ARMS OF ABERDEEN

ABERDEEN. UNION STREET LOOKING WEST.

The impressive building on the right is today better known as Esslemont and Macintosh, the city's renowned department store, but when this picture was taken at the beginning of this century it was called the Free Press Buildings. In 1922 the *Free Press* amalgamated with *Aberdeen Journal* (founded 1748) to become the *Aberdeen Press and Journal* and Scotland's oldest newspaper.

A sentimental view of the east end of Union Street before the First World War. Tram No. 54 was the first of the fleet to be fitted with a top cover to help keep the passengers on the upper deck dry. This tram was still in operation in 1951, forty years after its inaugural journey.

The Municipal and County Buildings have claims to be considered one of the finest structures in Scotland. The style is known as modern Gothic and Peddie & Kinnear of Edinburgh erected the buildings in 1873, at a cost of £80,000. To our civic forefathers, the new Town House represented everything that was good about Victorian Aberdeen with its wealth and growing confidence. The other fine building in the picture is the Athenaeum, designed in 1819 by Archibald Simpson for use as a reading room, but later to become the acclaimed restaurant known as 'Jimmy Hay's', until the building was burned out in 1973. Although restored, the restaurant was replaced as offices.

A group of fashionable citizens get ready to board a charabanc at the Castle Street stance for a day out in 1927.

Drivers and conductors waiting for their next route was a familiar sight in the Castlegate until 1974, when all the buses became operated by one man. In the background is the Salvation Army Citadel, whose architect, James Soutta, was clearly influenced by Balmoral Castle.

Castlegate in the 1920s certainly seemed vibrant but time brings changes. The twin-gabled house on the right, advertising Lipton's Tea, was demolished in 1935. It was known as Rolland's Lodging and dated from the sixteenth century. The statue of George, 5th Duke of Gordon, was moved to Golden Square in 1952. Perhaps the greatest change, however, is the volume of people actually using the Castlegate.

This early 1960 scene of a bus advertising cigarettes is today probably politically incorrect. The Mercat Cross has stood in the Castlegate since 1842, the heart of the city, and has been the setting for many events including Aberdeen's last public hanging in 1857 of a John Booth, condemned for the murder of his mother-in-law. The bus in the picture was nearing the end of its working life as it was withdrawn from the service in 1963.

Three
City Landmarks

The art gallery was formally opened in 1885 by Lord Provost Matthews and was designed by the architect, A. Marshall Mackenzie. It was one of the first buildings in Aberdeen to be built of coloured granite and cost £11,250. This picture was taken in 1910 before the addition of the war memorial and the subsequent demolition of the round tower at the far end of the gallery. The statue to the right is of General Gordon of Khartoum, the hero of the fight against the Dervishes in Sudan in 1885.

In 1905, the art gallery was extended to include a sculpture gallery; the balcony being supported by eighteen granite columns, many of which were donated by the Aberdeen Granite Traders Association. Guests from throughout Europe, who were later dined at the Town House by the Provost, attended the opening event. James Murray, the chairman of the gallery, was able to acquire 235 plaster casts of the world's finest sculptures.

The war memorial was designed by A. M. Mackenzie at a cost of £80,000, raised by public subscription. King George V and Queen Mary opened the building in 1925. The granite lion that sits proudly facing towards Union Terrace Gardens, was the work of the Aberdeen sculptor William Macmillan, who also designed the First World War victory medal. The architect, A.M. Mackenzie, lost his youngest son in 1916 during the First World War.

A group sitting under the imposing statue of William Wallace. Erected in 1888 and standing upon a massive granite base with his hand grasping his huge sword, a fitting pose for the warrior who in life fought so nobly for his beloved Scotland. In 1916 they had yet to discover *Braveheart*.

The bronze statue of Robert Burns was the work of Henry Bainsmith and was unveiled in 1892 by David Masson, an Aberdonian and a professor of rhetoric at Edinburgh University. Robert Burns, the national poet of Scotland, died in 1796 of endocarditis, induced by rheumatism at the age of thirty-seven. In his hand should be a daisy, but it has been vandalized so often that replacement became too expensive.

The Grand Hotel,
Aberdeen.

The Grand Hotel is now better known as the Caledonian Hotel. John Morgan, Aberdeen's master builder, built it in 1892 to a design by A. Marshall Mackenzie. It overlooks Union Terrace and Gardens, also the work of Morgan and Mackenzie. The Grand became the Caledonian in 1931.

If any hotel was likely to be described as 'grand' it was the Gordon House Hotel in Rubislaw Den North. Built in 1881 it was originally known as Rubislawden House and from this view could easily be mistaken as a castle. Today, the building is used as a nursing home.

The Marcliffe Hotel was a popular venue for functions in Aberdeen and was a landmark in the west end of the city. This impressive building lies empty but at least the name of the hotel has survived even if outside the city's boundaries.

Atholl Hotel, Aberdeen

C. 727

Aberdeen has many fine buildings, but the art of using granite comes closest to perfection with structures like the Atholl Hotel. Built in 1860 with a wing added in 1880, it exudes confidence and romance, a superb legacy of the skills of a bygone era. Was this building the inspiration for Marischal College?

The Northern Hotel, built in 1938 by A.G.R. (the son of A. Marshall) Mackenzie, is a complete contrast to the Atholl Hotel in the use and design of granite. Best described as 'Art Deco' in style, it was at one time the most sophisticated hotel in town, with a ballroom that was second to none. This 1949 view of the hotel makes the granite appear cold and austere.

George Gordon Byron was born in London in 1788, but spent the first ten years of his life in his mother's lodgings in Aberdeen. His mother, a Scottish heiress, was deserted by her husband, Captain 'Mad Jack' Byron, who spent her fortune. Byron attended the Grammar School, then in Schoolhill, until 1798, when he succeeded to the title of the 6th Lord Byron upon the death of his great-uncle. He left Aberdeen to continue his education at Harrow and Cambridge, building his reputation as the 'Byronic hero.' The statue of Lord Byron was erected in the grounds of the present Grammar School in 1923.

Before the Victoria Bridge opened in 1881, a ferryboat was used to transport people from the city to Torry. On 5 April 1876, the ferry was busy with Aberdonians enjoying a trip on the water on this public holiday. Disaster struck when the overloaded ferry capsized and thirty-two men, women and children tragically drowned. Despite a public outcry at the time, it took five years before the bridge was built.

The Wellington Suspension Bridge or 'Chain Briggie' was the link between Ferryhill and Torry until 1983, when a new bridge was constructed to cope with increased traffic. In 1914, when this photograph was taken, traffic was not a problem as this solitary horse and cart reveals.

Woolmanhill has been the site of an infirmary since 1741, but the building that we recognize today is work of Archibald Simpson, completed in 1839 at a cost of £16,700 and capable of accommodating 230 patients. Later additions were made in 1892. Woolmanhill has long since been surpassed as the city's principal hospital but remains an architectural gem.

Professor Matthew Hay, Medical Officer of Health, was the inspiration behind a plan to build a new hospital complex at Foresterhill, then on the suburbs of the city. It was financed by a public fund-raising campaign that raised £400,000. The Duke and Duchess of York opened the new Aberdeen Royal Infirmary in 1936. This aerial view of the hospital highlights how remote Foresterhill was when the project was conceived.

Morningfield Hospital was built in 1883, at a cost of £7,000, as a hospital for incurables. This view in 1905 would be impossible to reproduce as dwelling houses have since been built on the grounds. The hospital is still in use but it must be many years since a horse and carriage stood at the entrance.

Old Mill Hospital opened in 1907 as a hospital for the poor. It was used as a military hospital during the war, but for many years it was known as a hospital for the destitute and people had a fear of ending their days at Old Mill. It was reopened as Woodend Hospital in 1927 and gradually the stigma of the original name faded. This 1916 photograph was taken when the hospital was used to nurse the war wounded back to fitness and a return to the front line.

Crown Street was laid out with a deliberate curve to avoid the need to bridge Windmill Brae. This 1928 photograph captures the skill of the architect James Cumming Wyness, who successfully designed a building that would compliment the bend of the street. Built in 1907, the General Post Office stands majestically facing towards Union Street. No longer used by the postal service, there are proposals for the building to be given a new lease of life.

A fire engine sits at the entrance of the Aberdeen Central Fire Brigade Station sometime in 1939. The fire station was opened in 1899 by Baillie Lyon, who later became Lord Provost. Horses pulled the first fire engines. Opposite the station can be seen one of the many granite works that were located along King Street.

Almost hidden amidst the multi-storey St Nicholas House and the rear entrance to Marks & Spencer, is a house described as 'the jewel in the heart of the city.' George Skene, a wealthy merchant and Provost of Aberdeen, had the mansion built in 1669. This photograph was taken before the surrounding buildings were demolished. Fortunately, Provost Skene's House remained and was conserved and reopened as a museum in 1953 by the Queen Mother.

In 1746 the Duke of Cumberland was sent by his father George II to crush the Jacobite rising. He occupied Provost Skene House for six weeks on his way to Culloden to defeat Bonnie Prince Charlie's army. The house was located in a street known as Guest Row, at one time the smartest district in the city where all of the upper class lived. Unfortunately the area gradually fell into decline and Guest Row disappeared in a huge slum clearance programme in the 1930s.

In 1886 there was great disapproval when 'Jameson's Castle' was demolished as part of improvement to Schoolhill. The house had been built in 1586 by Andrew Jameson and had become a local landmark renowned for its turrets. A row of tenements was then built at the side of the now wider Schoolhill. The son of the builder, George Jameson, was a renowned portrait painter whose work included a portrait of Charles I. He lived and worked in this house until his death in 1644. The development of the Bon-Accord Centre in 1987, over a century later, met with equally vociferous opposition.

In 1964 a major redevelopment of the Nethergate gave the city a new store but led to the relocation of Aberdeen's most singular building, the Wallace Tower, to Tillydrone. Built in the sixteenth-century by Sir Robert Benholm, it was also known as Benholm's Tower. The distinguishing feature of the building must be the figure of the knight in the recess in the tower. Popular belief was that the figure was an effigy of William Wallace. The building was later used as a public house, but any publican with an eye to profit was certain to prefer the name of Wallace rather than Benholm.

Castlehill had been the site of a castle since around 1150 but over the centuries, as the city expanded, the castle was reduced in size until in 1794 military barracks were built within the walls. In this picture, taken in 1905, the barracks were the home of the Gordon Highlanders. In 1935 the regiment moved out to the Bridge of Don and the barracks were converted into flats. The flats were demolished and since 1965 the eighteen-storey Marischal Court has stood guard over Aberdeen.

GORDON BARRACKS, ABERDEEN.   A.5481.

The Gordon Barracks at the Bridge of Don was the home of the regiment for twenty-five years until they closed in 1960. In 1942, during an air raid, the barracks were badly damaged and twenty-seven soldiers lost their lives.

Miss Elizabeth Crombie Duthie gifted the Duthie Park to the City in 1883. To commemorate her generosity a statue of Hygeia, the goddess of health, was erected. Hygeia stands on top of a fluted column, guarded by four lions and overlooking all forty-two acres of parkland.

The engineer Robert Stevenson was responsible for the construction of twenty-three Scottish lighthouses for the Board of Northern Lighthouses, including the one at Girdleness which was completed in 1833. It stands 130 feet high and is visible for nineteen nautical miles. Stevenson's grandson was Robert Louis Stevenson, the famous author.

Torry did not become part of the city until 1891, and when this photograph was taken in 1905, Old Torry was a small fishing community. This view of Sinclair Road would be unrecognizable today and the only structures that remain are the leading lights, built in 1842 to help guide the boats into the harbour.

King Edward VII waited sixty years before finally becoming king in 1901. His reign was short and he died in 1910, but he was considered to have been a successful monarch who brought flair and vitality to the throne. The unveiling of his statue on 31 October 1914 attracted a crowd of over 20,000. The statue of his father, Prince Albert, had to be moved along Union Terrace to make way for Edward.

Four

Up Your Street

The only activities on this day in Ashley Road in 1915 were the children coming home from school. One young messenger boy who had taken a rest from his deliveries appears in this photograph. The name Ashley can be traced back to the nineteenth century when the district was covered in ash trees. Ashley Road School, built in 1888, is behind the trees on the right.

Belvidere Street came into existence in the 1880s and was named after a house owned by John Ewing of Shelagreen, who lived in the locality. At the end of the street are gates leading to Victoria Park and a view of the fountain. The sight of only one car in the street would be a remarkable occasion today!

In the days before the First World War, living in Bonnymuir Place was considered to be like living in the countryside. The street was laid out in 1890, on grounds once belonging to the University. Wm. S Ray, a tea, wine and spirit merchant, opened in 1904 and remained in business until it became the American Food Store in 1974.

58

Little has changed in Carlton Place since this photograph was taken in 1920. A typical west end row of granite built houses that have stood the test of time. The street is empty apart from a horse and cart heading towards the camera. Some things have changed at least!

Old Aberdeen has been part of the city since 1891 and today it is littered with houses occupied by university staff. The Chanonry is a tree-lined avenue of Georgian houses, each being a masterpiece. In this turn of the century photograph of two children standing in front of St Machar's Cathedral you can almost hear the birds chirping, it seems so peaceful.

Claremount Road can claim to be in the west end of the city, but the boy standing on his own in the middle of the road is in bare feet. Standards of living for many were low and some families lived in slums. In the late nineteenth century, the city quickly expanded with the escalation of residential suburbs, but many people remained trapped in poverty.

The two boys in this picture of Desswood Place in 1913 not only have boots but they each have their own bicycle. The street was named after Alexander Davidson of Desswood, who was chairman of the Land Association, on whose land the street was laid out. The Land Association was responsible for many of the streets built in the west end of the city.

Don Street consists of houses dating from the seventeenth and eighteenth centuries, and tenements from the end of the nineteenth century. It is a street of immense character and adds to the appeal of Old Aberdeen. The children in this photograph, taken in the 1930s, are able to play in the narrow street, distracted by only the occasional car. Thanks to considerable conservation, the street has managed to retain a great deal of its past heritage.

This view of the High Street, Old Aberdeen, with the Town House at the far end, dates from the 1930s. The architect George Jaffrey built the Georgian Town House in 1788. Until 1891, when Old Aberdeen merged with the city, the Town House was the administration building for the borough, which even had its own Provost and was truly independent

The tenement block in Elm Place is rather stylish with turrets at each gable end. The view from the windows in the beginning of the last century would have been of the meal mills that operated in Berryden. Wm Beattie, the grocer on the corner, opened in 1906, but sold his business to Duncan Stewart in 1923. The last decade has seen a number of changes and Berryden is now one large retail park.

Forest Avenue was until 1896, known as South Forest Road, but the Town Council thought the name long winded and a change was made. This 1912 view is typical of the period; an almost deserted street except for a couple of horses and carts. The vacant land to the right of the photograph has been filled in with houses.

In 1911 Fountainhall Road was clearly an affluent neighbourhood. Note the elegantly dressed women and the elderly gentleman with the white hat and walrus moustache. In 1876, when the street was first laid out it was called North St Swithin Street, but perhaps not too surprisingly the name was soon changed. The name Fountainhall is taken from a nearby mansion dating back to 1753. Today it is the City District Authority, with recommendations from the property developer and the support of the Lord Provost and local councillors, the emergency services and head postmaster incorporated, who decide street names. It certainly seems comprehensive! A Chivas Brothers wagon is making deliveries to the tea, wine and spirit merchant on the corner of Beaconsfield Place. A tram, with an advertisement for Bovril, makes its way down Fountainhall Road towards Castle Street. The main depot for the tramway system was located in Fountainhall Road and at its peak, accommodated seventy-five trams. The depot was eventually sold to Grampian Television in 1960.

A view of Gray Street from 1909 and again we see a solitary horse and cart in an otherwise deserted street. This uniform terrace of granite-built houses has remained more or less unaltered since they were erected in the late nineteenth century. The boom in house building to cater for the increasing middle classes continued until the outbreak of war in 1914. The day of the horse and cart would also be numbered with the onset of mass production of motor vehicles needed for the war effort.

A young boy is strolling down Laurelwood Avenue with a canister of milk in his hand as two stone lions watch from the garden of the house on the left. Life in 1911 seems so tranquil.

James Emslie opened Loanhead Quarry in 1730. Rubislaw opened in 1741. The Wrights and Coopers Incorporation in the 1870s laid out Loanhead Terrace and although the name is taken from the quarry, the actual quarry was nearer to Mile End and Craigie Loanings. This 1909 photograph was taken long before any alterations to the dormer windows were considered.

Torry became part of the City in 1891, only a few years after trawl fishing began in earnest. To house the many newcomers who sought employment in the nascent fishing industry, the small village of Torry rapidly became a community of tenements. Menzies Road on a day in 1915 was a hub of activity as a crowd gathered in front of the Victoria Bar keen to get themselves included in the photograph. The street was named after the Menzie family who until 1875 owned most of the land south of the river.

Mid Stocket Road is built on land that was once the royal hunting forest of Stocket, and was bestowed to the city in 1313 by Robert the Bruce. The towering spire of Beechgrove church dominates this scene. Only a mere six hundred years before this picture was taken, wolves would have roamed the forest in search of food.

Queen's Road in 1909 was the residence of the wealthy and confirmation that Aberdeen was a city of prosperity. The street has an abundance of individual houses and it was here that A. Marshall Mackenzie and John Morgan, the leading figures in architecture and construction, had their own homes built. In order to keep the street in a straight line; several older houses were demolished.

A group of ladies are seen cycling along Riverside Road one day in 1913. It was all the rage for ladies of a certain upbringing to indulge in this new craze. The style of dress must have made this pursuit somewhat awkward, but it was in vogue and even fun.

Riverside Road was certainly the place to try out the latest fad. Private motor cars were scarce on the ground in 1909, and by 1938 there were only 5,500 private cars licensed in the city. The normal mode of transport was at best the tramcar or a bicycle. At least the driver and passengers are dressed appropriately for their run past the gates at the Duthie Park. Hopefully, they will not meet a group of lady cyclists around the next corner.

Rosemount came into existence in 1829 and, named, as so often a custom of the time, after a house already in the neighbourhood. Rosemount Place has always been a busy thoroughfare and until 1954 was part of the tramway system. This early view makes clear that Rosemount with its own peculiar mix of architecture is an area full of character and individuality.

The Morgan Buildings in St Swithin Street were described as the most sophisticated tenements of the time. Built in 1895 at the height of the tenement boom, they were one of the first tenements built privately for rental. Aberdeen tenements normally had two things in common – granite built and poor plumbing.

The Incorporated Trades laid out Thomson Street in 1879 and, like many of the neighbouring streets, the builder was John Morgan. In fact he had a house built for him and his family overlooking Victoria Park. The street was named after a James Thomson who was involved in managing the widows fund for the Incorporated Trades. In 1886 the Morgan family moved to 50 Queen's Road, a house that confirmed that John Morgan had made it to the top.

Union Grove in the early days of the twentieth-century and not a vehicle in site! Although a street of tenements, it has always had an air of grandeur and the tenants knew that they lived in the west end. Union Grove took its name from a house owned by a Provost Hadden in whose land the street was built..

The corner of Union Grove and St Swithin Street has always been busy with children heading to or from Ashley Road School. Today a lollipop lady would be on hand to look after the children but in 1912 traffic was never a problem. The continuation of Union Grove leads to Cromwell Road; given this name because the developers thought Union Grove was already long enough and a different named street would be easier to market.

The Town Council built the first council tenement-housing scheme in 1897 in Urquhart Road. The houses were mainly occupied by the workers from the local granite works and at the far end of the street the cranes from one of the granite yards can be seen. The street was named after Baillie Robert Urquhart, who as chairman of the Land Association, was responsible for many of the streets built in Aberdeen from 1875 onwards.

Five
Earning a Living

Aberdeen's expansion as a fishing port was built on herring. The herring drifters, the Fifies and Zulus, were sailing vessels with masts as long as the boat itself. In the background is a steam trawler, first introduced in 1882 and destined to help make Aberdeen the country's biggest fishing port. The Round House at Footdee can just be seen behind the trawler. By the mid-1930s the herring boom was over.

Two horse-drawn carts are waiting to be loaded with bags of coal from a 'coalie' boat at the head of the harbour. In 1908 the horse was an essential form of transport, as a glance along Regent Quay would confirm. The working day of a coal dockworker was long and hard, unloading coal shipped from Blyth on Tyneside to keep the steam trawlers at sea.

ANI. THE QUAY AND CUSTOM HOUSE, ABERDEEN.

This 1930 view of Regent Quay features the Harbour Offices, designed by A. Marshall Mackenzie in 1883, with a clock tower that appears out of proportion. It was conceived in this manner so that the clock could be seen anywhere in the harbour area. The premises of John Taylor, rope and twine manufacturer, is to the left of the harbour offices. Today, oil dominates the harbour.

In 1909, half of the fish trade in Scotland was landed at Aberdeen. New fish markets had been constructed at the north side of the Albert Basin and thanks to the arrival of the railway in 1850, the fish could be transported to almost anywhere in the country. There was no shortage of fish in 1909.

Another scene of the fish market, but this time twenty years later. The fish market had seen few changes and the industry continued to boom. In the 1930s, Aberdeen had over 350 trawlers in operation and until 1955 the fishing industry was the city's largest employer. The trawler fleets all but vanished in 1980 as a result of the National Dock Labour Board restrictions and the fishing fleet moved to Peterhead.

To work in a fish house you had to become acclimatized to the smells and be able to work in the cold as central heating had yet to be invented. These fish quines appear to be a contented group of girls with hands and arms stained by working in the smokey house where the fish were smoked over a peat pit.

A different group of workers but the same boss as in the previous photograph. Note his collar and tie and the watch fob. To catch fish, the trawlermen needed nets, and it was mainly the work of young women who used wooden needles to braid the nets. It was unusual for married women to go out to work and even as late as the 1950s many firms would not employ married women. At least net making was a job a married woman could do at home.

The Round House, Footdee, is a perfect backdrop for the Fittie ferry. It seems incredible that the ferry was still in use until the 1930s. In this 1910 view, the ferryman is taking his passenger from Footdee, across the mouth of the harbour, to Old Torry. Footdee as we know it today, was part of an improvement by the Town Council in 1809 to the harbour area, and the fishermen and their families were moved to purpose built squares of terraced dwellings. John Smith, the city architect, was responsible for the design but the name given to the scheme, Fish Town, was soon abandoned. Fittie is unique in many ways.

Two young shop assistants stand on the step of the premises of their employer, Patrick Burr, pharmacist, at the corner of Mid-Stocket Road and Mile-End Avenue. The photograph was taken in 1929 with a window display for Pepsodent. Mr Burr opened the shop in 1903 and remained in business until 1936.

Allans Public Supply Stores had twelve branches throughout the city, including this one at the corner of Broomhill Road and Holburn Road. This photograph was taken in 1908 and the name above the door is Duncan, and may be the name of the woman in the picture. Whatever the explanation is, this is a good example of what a corner shop really was like, long before supermarkets were considered necessary.

JACOB'S LADDER, WOODSIDE, ABERDEEN 159

Until an economic crisis in the mid-nineteenth century, the textile industry was the biggest employer in Aberdeen with 12,000 men, women and children working in factories either in the city centre or at Donside. Jacob's ladder were the steps that took 1,200 workers from their homes in Woodside down to the bridge and across to the Grandholm Mills. How many of these workers' coats in 1924 were made from Crombie cloth?

418. Grandholm Bridge from Jacob's Ladder "Adelphi Series"

Grandholm Mills is famous for Crombie cloth but less known for its radical approach in providing for its workforce. Even in the days of the Depression in the 1930s, the workers were paid sickness benefit, holiday pay and there was a pension scheme. Unfortunately, this did not prevent the factory firm reducing the workforce as the Depression bit deeper and the demand for cloth diminished.

This photograph of the shop and staff of George Greig gives you an idea of how diversified a shopkeeper had to be in 1909. The window on the left is advertising his wares as an agricultural seedsman, while the window on the right is selling Greigs old blended whisky. In fact he was a tea, wine and general merchant, and was in business from 1895 to 1919. These premises at the corner of Ellon Road and Links Road are now a bank.

The Broadford Works of Richards Limited were at one time the largest single employer in Aberdeen. They specialized in the manufacture of linen, canvas and sailcloth, and were the one of only two textile companies in the city to have survived from the last century. Here in 1912, a number of women mill workers, known as 'shawlies', can be seen amongst these workers.

Markets have been held in the Green since the Middle Ages. Friday was the day when the country people would come to sell their fresh vegetables, fruit and dairy produce to the 'Townees'. Overlooking this busy 1900s scene is the 'Mannie Well', an ancient monument that has had several homes and was moved from the Green in 1958. It is now resident in the Castlegate. The Green, the borough's first settlement, has almost vanished as a result of numerous developments.

The Whitefield Dairy was based in Baker Street from 1902 until 1930. Here we can see a proud work force standing in front of the company's first motor vehicle, with milk churns already loaded in the rear. In the background, a horseshoe is nailed to the shed; a reminder of how they used to deliver the milk.

A dairyman from the Whitefield Dairy can be seen delivering milk in Belmont Street sometime in 1904. James Hay was a tailor and clothier in Belmont Street until 1905. In the basement was the Thistle Hall, a mission hall for the deaf and dumb. This milkman does not look too happy; perhaps he has been overlooked for the motor run.

C. M. Smith opened his drapers shop at 78 Holburn Street in 1925, but by 1926 the business was closed and a fishmonger took over the premises. The staff in this photograph probably assumed a longer employment but you can bet that the present trader will last longer in business.

This photograph was taken in 1904, the year that Mr Birnie opened his pharmacy at 361 Holburn Road. The window display is advertising 'Quinine Iron Tonic', which was presumably good for you. Would either of the two gentlemen standing in the doorway have thought that the business would continue to operate until 1942 when another chemist would take over?

A motorman and his conductor pose on board the No. 15 tramcar in front of Mannofield church in 1910. The Mannofield tram route opened in 1902 and was in business until 1951. An early form of 'pay as you enter' was trailed in 1914, whereby the conductor would stand on the rear platform and collect the fares as the passengers boarded the tramcar. The Mannofield passengers, who sent the Town Council a petition demanding that this system be dropped, did not appreciate this radical change. The fare-paying passengers won the day and 'pay as you enter' was aborted. Mannofield was the site of a depot for trams and buses for almost one hundred years before closing in 1958.

Salmon fishing has been an occupation for Aberdonians since the fishing rights were granted to the city by Robert the Bruce in 1313. In this photograph, taken at the turn of the century, the fishermen are busy landing their catch on the River Dee at the Esplanade. In the background can be seen the premises of Richard W. Lewis & Sons, boat-builder, The Universal Fish Supply Company, and Williamson & Company. How many salmon could be landed from this particular stretch of the Dee today?

Aberdeen will always be identified with granite. The granite would be taken from the quarry and transported to a granite yard where the stone would be dressed, polished and then the mason would sculpture the granite into the required monument. Today there are only three companies in business in Aberdeen. Loanhead Quarry in Rosemount was the first ever quarry in Aberdeen and opened ten years before Rubislaw.

The responsibilities of a policeman increased rapidly with the growth of traffic. Long before the invention of traffic lights, a policeman would have to be on duty at a busy junction to ensure the safety of pedestrians and road users. In this photograph, taken in the early years of this century, policeman No.41 can be seen at the top of Union Street and Market Street, calmly directing traffic. He seems unconcerned as a tramcar heads towards him and is clearly in control.

The New Market was built in 1842 by Archibald Simpson and was Aberdeen's first covered arcade. Practically everything was on sale inside this huge market hall, almost a hundred yards long, with shops in aisles on two floors. The facade on Market Street has been described as a masterpiece, but this did not prevent the building from being demolished in 1971 and replaced by a shopping centre. In this photograph you can almost imagine the smells and odours from all the different produce on sale.

Six

Education, Salvation and Damnation

The election of the rector of Aberdeen University has always been a serious event. In 1902 the Rt Hon Charles Ritchie, Privy Councilor and Chancellor of the Exchequer, sought election as rector. He was duly elected in 1903.

Marischal College was founded in 1593 by George, Fifth Earl of Marischal, as a Protestant rival to Kings College, Old Aberdeen. The building that we know today was designed by A. Marshall Mackenzie and built in 1905 as an extension to the old college. To make way for the granite frontage on Broad Street, Greyfriars Kirk was demolished in spite of a public outcry. The present Greyfriars church was built at the corner of Broad Street and Queen Street. In this 1927 photograph a rather dapper gentleman can be seen crossing Broad Street in front of a single deck bus. In the background, Marischal College, with an almost fretwork appearance, underlines the excellence of the skill of the architect.

Behind the granite facade of Marischal College are the buildings known as the quadrangle, built from 1837 to 1844 to a design by Archibald Simpson. Part of the 1905 changes involved raising the central tower to a height of 235 feet. The tower was extended from where the clock can be seen on the tower. This picture, taken in 1907, accentuates the newly built Mitchell Tower, named after Charles Mitchell, who donated almost half of the 1905 extension costs.

William Elphinstone, Bishop of Aberdeen, founded King's College in 1494. The Crown steeple of the chapel dates from 1504 and is considered to be an architectural gem. In the distance, a horse and cart can be seen making its way up from the Town House of Old Aberdeen. The two universities merged in 1860 to become the University of Aberdeen.

MIDDLE SCHOOL AND MARISCHAL COLLEGE, ABERDEEN

The Mitchell Tower dominates the skyline of Aberdeen and in this photograph it dwarfs the Middle School. The school was built in 1875 to a design by James Matthews and was originally called the Gallowgate School. The school had a swimming pool and was open to other schools to send their pupils to learn to swim. All this came to an end in 1975 with the closure of the school.

Ashley Road School was built in 1888 and designed by Jenkins and Marr. Constructed in granite from the Rubislaw and Kemnay quarries, it stands in grounds once known as Friendship Farm. These pupils from 1912 seem to be fascinated by the presence of the photographer.

The present Grammar School was built in 1863 and designed by James Matthews, who later became Lord Provost. The cost of £13,000 was funded from the Common Good Fund. When the old Grammar School at Schoolhill was demolished, a doorway and pediment was rebuilt into the north end of the new school. A fire in 1986 almost destroyed the school.

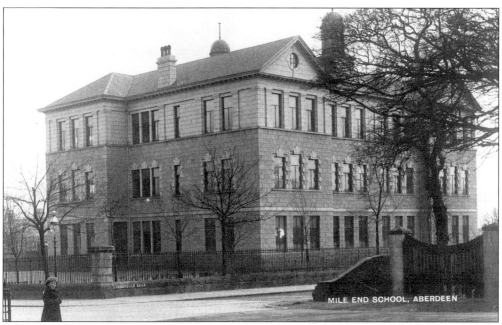

Mile End School is built on land once owned by the University of Aberdeen and was designed by Arthur H.L. Mackinnon at the turn of the century. This photograph demonstrates the fine standard of granite work applied to public buildings; granite will stand the test of time.

HILTON SCHOOL, ABERDEEN

Hilton Academy came into existence as part of a drive by the Town Council to provide housing in the years between the wars. Hilton Estate, built on 198 acres of land that was purchased for £22,000, was developed into a municipal housing estate. In the playground of the school stands the Hilton Stone or Langstane, an ancient monument dating from the Bronze Age.

ROBERT GORDON'S COLLEGE, ABERDEEN

Robert Gordon's College began life in 1730 as a hospital to educate fourteen poor boys and was founded by Robert Gordon, a rich merchant who made his fortune trading from Danzig in Poland. It became a boy's boarding school in 1750 and was substantially extended by John Smith in 1830. By the late 1880s it was no longer a school for the poor boys of the city, but became an independent school to educate the sons of Aberdeen's more affluent citizens.

John Smith was the architect responsible for building the Town's Schools in Little Belmont Street in 1841. In 1901 a row of Georgian houses in Schoolhill made way for what was to become the Central Higher Grade School. The school changed its name once again in 1954, when it became the Aberdeen Academy. The janitors of the old school lived in what is today known as James Dun's House in Schoolhill. This house was restored as a museum by the City Council in 1975, by which time the Academy had moved to Hazlehead. Following a period when the school had lain empty and somewhat forgotten, the Town's Schools was rejuvenated as a public house and the Central School converted into retail outlets. The ex-pupils would doubtlessly approve.

In 1837 Archibald Simpson designed Mrs Emslie's Institution or Female Orphan Asylum, in Albyn Place. It was to become better known as the High School for Girls, although in recent years it has had the benefit of further name changes. The school was evacuated and used as hospital for soldiers during the First World War.

William Smith built the Boy's and Girl's Hospital in King Street in 1869. Today the building houses Robert Gordon's Institute of Technology. When this photograph was taken in 1913, it was the School of Domestic Science. Long before anyone had considered the name 'Technology,' the Mechanic's Institute at 15 Market Street was created to teach apprentices the appropriate skills and crafts.

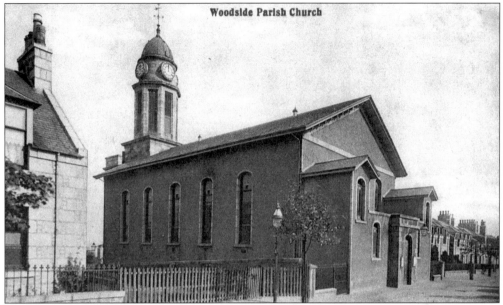

Woodside has been a part of the city since 1891, with a thriving community employed in the granite and textile industries. Almost hidden away in Church Street, is Woodside New Parish Church, built in 1846 by Archibald Simpson. The feature of the design is the clock tower and can be easily seen from Great Northern Road. Much has changed in Woodside since this photograph was taken in 1912.

The parish of St George's-in-the-West is in the part of the city that experienced major redevelopment in the late 1980s with the construction of the Bon-Accord Centre. The church in John Street closed in 1968 and has been used as a health club. Whatever happened to all those pews?

Trinity Congregational Church.

*Our Bazaar takes place in the Y.M.C.A.
Hall, on Friday and Saturday, 18th and 19th
curt., opening each day at 12 o'clock noon. I
expect to see you there.*

JCSmith

The Trinity congregational church is another church to have closed and the building put to another use. Built in 1876, it now forms part of the Maritime Museum in the Shiprow. The principal part of the museum is the sixteenth century Provost Ross's House, which was saved from ruin in 1954 and became the home of the museum in 1984. In 1904 the members of the congregation were being reminded to attend the church bazaar at the YMCA Hall.

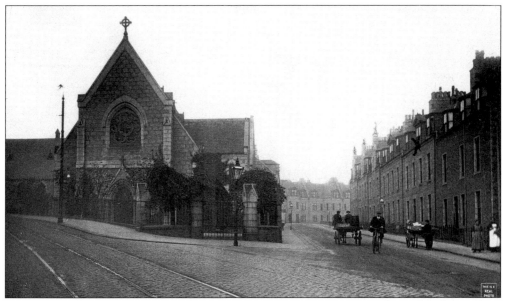

Ferryhill parish church is today better known as Caledonian Court. Built in 1877 by William Smith, it is has since been converted into flats. This view of Ferryhill Terrace in 1909 would now be inconceivable – there are no cars, only horses and carts and a man on a bicycle!

In the latter part of the nineteenth century, there was an outburst of religious building in Aberdeen, as rival denominations competed to erect bigger and grander places of worship. The Carden Place United Presbyterian Church exemplified this passion. The elder of the church, Robert Wilson, was also the architect and it was constructed in 1880. Today, the building is home to offices.

Built in 1896 by George Watt for the Free Church, Beechgrove church is another example of competitive and ambitious church building. The Free Church had broken away from the Established Church in 1843, and as their wealthy parishioners moved out to the new suburbs in the west end, it seemed appropriate to build a church that would reflect both their wealth and their religious convictions. Beechgrove church, with its spire that seems to rise into the heavens itself, is a fitting tribute to its architect.

ST MARYS CATHEDRAL, ABERDEEN.   11754

Bishop James Kyle was responsible for the founding of St Mary's church in 1860, which was built three hundred years after the Scottish Parliament had banned mass. In 1877 a two hundred-foot spire was added to help celebrate the church becoming a cathedral and also as a response to the frantic plans of other denominations. The architects and builders of the city were certainly kept busy by the clergy.

Not to be outdone, the Episcopalian Church, led by Rev. John Comper, erected St Margaret's Church in the Spital. Although not as grand as the other churches of the period, it does possess a certain aura. The convent was added in 1887, designed by the Reverend's son, Ninian Comper, who later received a knighthood for his work as a church architect..

When this photograph was taken in 1908, St Ninian's church stood almost alone at the top of Mid-Stocket Road – the Royal Infirmary at Foresterhill had yet to be conceived. The church was built in 1898 to a design by William Kelly, who was perhaps better known as the man who put the leopards, or Kelly's Cats, on Union Bridge. A vertical sundial can be seen to the right of the doorway, another example of the architect's creativity.

'Education, Salvation and Damnation' is the name given to the trio of civic buildings that dominate the north end of Union Terrace. The Central Library, representing education, was built in 1891 to a design by George Watt, who beat A.M. Mackenzie in a competition for the commission. The beaten finalist built the South United Free Church the following year. It has been described as a miniature of St Paul's Cathedral. Damnation would later be depicted by HM Theatre.

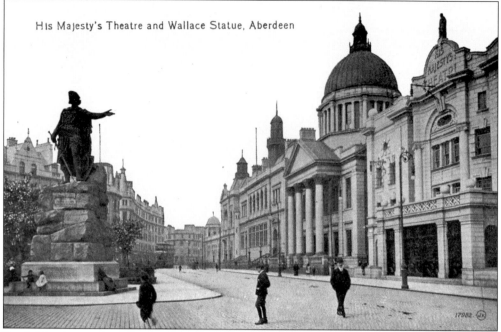

His Majesty's Theatre and Wallace Statue, Aberdeen

Frank Matcham, who specialized in the design of theatres, completed the trio in 1906 with the opening of His Majesty's Theatre. The frontage is white Kemnay granite with the remainder being built of pink Tilliefourie granite. The Wallace statue, erected eighteen years earlier, is by chance pointing across to the theatre entrance.

Guild Street was the venue for Aberdeen's own opera house in 1872. By the time this photograph was taken it had changed its name to Her Majesty's Theatre. The doors were closed in 1906 with the opening of His Majesty's Theatre, but it reopened under the much-loved name of the Tivoli in 1910. For the next fifty-six years it was to become the hub of live entertainment in the city.

Seven
Doon the Toon

An aerial view of the city centre, taken sometime in the 1950s. Marischal College and St Nicholas Kirk are obvious landmarks, but the real fun is to try and find your way around the city from this unusual angle.

Albyn Place, Aberdeen.

Albyn Place came into existence in the 1830s when Archibald Simpson began building a number of substantial villas on land owned by James Skene of Rubislaw, who lived in Edinburgh, in Albyn Place. James Skene clearly had an eye for the potential profit in property development. A glance at the Edwardian ladies walking towards the camera confirms how affluent you had to be to live in this street.

The clock tower of Christ's Church has observed several street names changes since it was built in 1850. The top of Union Street, until 1890, was called Union Place, and the top of Holburn Street was once known as Wellington Place. At least Alford Place has managed to remain a 'Place'.

The corner of Bridge Street and Union Street was the site of the Palace Hotel until it was destroyed in 1941 during an air raid. This photograph, taken in the early 1950s, shows the foundations of C & A being laid. On the opposite corner, above George Pegler's fruit shop, is another hotel, The Bridge Hotel, remaining in business until 1961.

Broad Street was at one time the foremost street in Aberdeen, but in 1902 it was almost totally removed to make way for the Marischal College facade. The street catered mainly for the needs of the college and as this photograph reveals, the College Gate Clothiery House could supply a best scotch tweed suit for sixty shillings – a real bargain. The main archway led you into Marischal College.

Crown Street was laid out in the early 1800s and can boast a number of fine buildings all completed at a later date. This 1950s view illustrates the skill of the architect George Coutts, who designed the Star and Garter building in 1899. The British Linen Bank and Bank of Scotland flank entry to the street.

The tramlines in this 1920s photograph vividly emphasize the curve in Crown Street; laid out in this manner to avoid bridging Windmill Brae. The turreted gable of the General Post Office building is so cleverly designed that the curve in the street is almost a feature. The Ferryhill tram route was closed in 1931.

19, Golden Square, Aberdeen.

The Hammermen Corporation of the Incorporated Trades, who were also responsible for Crown Street, built Golden Square in the 1820s. Legal action had to be taken in 1821 to force the residents to pay for their share of the garden railings. The railings have survived but the gardens have since become parking spaces. In the background, the spire of St Mary's Cathedral soars above all.

Guild Street was used as an overnight parking lot for tramcars (tarpaulins were thrown over the open-tops) until a depot was built in Torry in 1904. The street was named after Dr William Guild, who in 1631 donated a meeting hall to the Seven Incorporated Trades known as the Trinity Hall, and was originally built at 12-14 Guild Street. A public fountain was built at the corner of Guild Street and Market Street to commemorate Dr Guild's generosity.

The construction of King Street began in 1804. At the corner of Union Street and King Street, the 'hinge of the city,' is the Archibald Simpson designed North of Scotland bank. In order to make space for the bank, an inn was demolished in 1838. In the background, the tower of the North Kirk, now Aberdeen Arts Centre, rises to the sky. In 1905 when this photograph was taken, who would have guessed that the bank would revert back to being a tavern?

The electrification of the tramway lines in Aberdeen began in 1899 on the Woodside route. Until then the trams had been horse-drawn. Travelling by tram was considered a service for the better off; the cost of the fare (three old pence) was too high for the majority of people who simply walked everywhere. This photograph, taken in King Street, shows an empty tram, but perhaps the crew is posing for the photographer. In 1902 the first Sunday service was introduced amid a public outcry. However, the experiment proved popular and getting to church became easier. The horses in the picture were to become redundant in 1902 when the route was electrified and in 1989 Grampian Regional Transport was sold as part of privatization.

Market Street was laid out in 1842 and got its name from the New Market; both were built by Archibald Simpson. The street was always noisy, with huge Clydesdale horses pulling their heavy loads up from the docks, on to Union Street and on to wherever. Market Street was considered so steep that there was reluctance to route a tram in case of brake failure. You can almost hear the noise from the horses' hooves in this 1906 photograph.

Queen's Cross is today known as the home of Queen Victoria, or rather her statue. When this photograph was taken almost ninety years ago, a rather ornate tram-cum-lamp-post was in her place. The architect responsible for the design of Rubislaw church was J. Russell Mackenzie who went bankrupt, it was alleged, because of his wife's high living. They immigrated to South Africa in 1883.

The Royal Insurance building was built in 1911 by George Bennett Mitchell and is noted for the octagonal tower and dome. At first glance it resembles the 'Monkey House' building at the corner of Union Terrace. In the background can be seen the spire of St Mary's Cathedral.

James Skene, of Rubislaw, completed his property enterprise when in 1852 he had Mackenzie and Matthews design the majestic and most expensive street in the west end of the city. Rubislaw Terrace is a true terrace – the houses alternate in pairs and overlook communal gardens. In 1915, only the most affluent and sophisticated lived here.

By the early 1950s, the Upperkirkgate had seen a fair amount of change. Slum buildings in the Guestrow had began to be demolished and plans were in place for bringing the Civic buildings into the twentieth century with St Nicholas House as the centrepiece of modern architecture. All that would remain would be Provost Skene's House. St Nicholas Centre was yet to be envisaged.

This photograph from the early years of the century has everything. An open-top tram heading towards Woodside; hand pushed carts, loaded with goods; shops with canvas canopies and women dressed in their Edwardian elegance. But the biggest change must be the Upperkirkgate. It looks so long and narrow as it leads up to Marischal College. Most of the buildings to the right of the picture were to disappear in the 1930s.

A slightly later scene of a street that no longer exists. The corner of St Nicholas Street and the Nethergate was for many years the site of Morrison's Economic Stores, owned by Jimmy Mearns. In time it was to become Marks & Spencer's first store in the city, but that was before the emergence of the St Nicholas Centre in 1967.

St Nicholas Street and George Street could boast a number of good local stores. Reid & Pearson, Isaac Benzies, the Equitable and the Rubber Shop were just a few of the names that were to become almost legendary long before shopping malls arrived in Aberdeen. The Woodside tram can be seen passing Hepworths the tailors, sometime in the early 1950s. The last tram from Woodside ran in 1955.

Eight

Loose Ends

The King and Queen at Holburn Station

King Edward VII and Queen Alexandra opened the extension of Marischal College on the 27 September 1906, on the occasion of the University Quarter-centenary celebrations. The King arrived at Holburn Street station and travelled in procession through the city, watched by over 200,000 people.

The splendour of the occasion is vividly brought to life in this picture of the King, sitting in an open carriage pulled by four white horses. The crowds were able to get a close up view of the King and Queen as the royal party made their way along Forest Avenue.

The total cost of the Marischal College extensions was £180,000. Almost half of the amount was donated by the Mitchell Bequest to help finance a graduation hall and the extension to the central tower. Not surprisingly, both of these structures were named after their benefactor. To make way for the facade of the college, Greyfriars Kirk (built in 1530) was demolished. The new Greyfriars church was erected at the corner of Broad Street and Queen Street.

KÖNIG EDUARD BEI DER 400 JAHRFEIER DER SCHOTTISCHEN UNIVERSITÄT ABERDEEN.

[4] 263
20.10.06.

Lord Roberts was given the honour of welcoming the members of the royal party as they arrived at the entrance to Marischal College. The guests were certainly given the red carpet treatment that day. Lord Roberts had retired as commander-in-chief of the Army in 1904.

Lord Roberts at Aberdeen. Inspecting the Royal Artillery. T.F.

Holmes
Silver City Series.

The 27 September 1906 was a busy day for Lord Roberts. The mounted troops of the Royal Artillery are lined up in front of the music hall, ready for inspection. Born in 1832, Frederick Roberts won the Victoria Cross during the Indian Mutiny and he became the country's most decorated soldier. Created a Lord in 1892, he rose through the ranks to become commander-in-chief in 1901. He died in 1914 while visiting troops in France.

Union Street, looking Eastward

Aberdeen has never seen celebrations to match the opening of the extension to Marischal College. A bedecked Union Street is crowded with people enjoying the festivities. For four days the city commemorated the occasion with numerous events. Everyone was in the mood for revelry!

Market Street to Castle Street

The statue of Queen Victoria looks over the scenes of merriment as the citizens of Aberdeen welcome her son Edward VII to the opening of the world's second largest granite building, Marischal College. Would she have been amused with the proceedings?

The Salvation Army Band from Bridgeton is on the march in Guild Street in 1927. The passengers on the tram to Torry have to follow patiently behind. In the background are the Waverley and Balmoral Hotels, both built in 1870.

These soldiers from the Salvation Army Barracks are lined up for a group photograph of the silver band of 1918. The Band of Hope meetings in the Citadel provided an opportunity to sing along with the band and to hear bible readings from one of the officers. It was considered to be a rousing evening's entertainment.

In 1837 the city architect John Smith designed a meeting place for the Faculty of Advocates. By 1898 the lawyers had moved to new premises and the building was refurbished as a restaurant, the Queen's Rooms. This grand and elegant restaurant closed in 1910 with the coming of the cinema, and for the next seventy years the Queen's Cinema occupied this handsome building.

Watt and Grant's Store was in business at the corner of Union Street and Dee Street for ninety-nine years. To make room for the luncheon and tearooms, the roof of the building was raised. The store closed in 1981 and today part of the building is again being used as a venue to satisfy the appetites of the locals, albeit at a different pace.

Tearooms were very much in fashion at the beginning of the twentieth century and in 1907, Sangster and Henderson's new tearooms at 32 Union Street were the height of sophistication.

In 1914 La Scala was opened as the city's first purpose-built cinema. To compliment the cinema, tearooms were incorporated into the design. The all-star programme included a showing of *The Little Minister* and seats could be booked for one shilling. La Scala closed in 1935 when it was to become the Majestic Cinema.

BOYS' BAND, NAZARETH HOUSE, ABERDEEN.

Nazareth House was a home for orphan and unfortunate children of the Catholic faith. This photograph, taken in 1944 in the grounds of the home, is of the boy's band. The priests and nuns who ran the home had to rely upon the generosity of others to provide for the children. Life may have been difficult, but if the faces of the boys are a measurement, there was still a lot to be happy about. They were probably the neatest and best-equipped band in town.

SENIOR GIRLS, NAZARETH HOUSE, ABERDEEN.

Another photograph taken in the same year but this time involving the senior girls from Nazareth House. Individuality was clearly not an option for these young ladies.

BABY BOYS, NAZARETH HOUSE, ABERDEEN.

Nazareth House had to cater for children of all ages. It may be somewhat of a surprise but the children in this photograph are all boys. The style of haircut would suggest that one of the nuns was given the task of hairdresser.

The *Demosthenes* was a cargo passenger ship built in 1911 by Harland & Wolff, Belfast, but registered in Aberdeen for the White Star Line. An Alfred Middleton, assistant electrician, joined the crew of the *Demosthenes* in August 1911 for her maiden voyage to Brisbane. After that trip he was appointed to the *Titanic*. Middleton died in the sinking, and his body was never recovered. The fate of the *Demosthenes* was less dramatic and she was eventually sold for scrap in 1931. The identities of these passengers are unknown but the photograph was taken en route to Australia.

The Timmer Market was held each year in the Castlegate on the last Wednesday of August and traditionally sold wooden goods and toys. Peashooters or pluffers were the great attraction for children. In 1935 the market was moved to Justice Street but the venue is of little consequence; the real ritual was the timber or timmer wares.

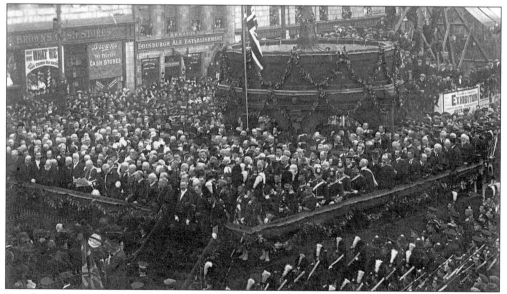

On the 10 May 1910, in towns and villages throughout the land, crowds gathered for the proclamation of King George V. Aberdeen was no different and thousands gathered at the Mercat Cross to hear the proclamation of King George V's accession to the throne. George succeeded his father, Edward VII, who had reigned for only nine years. 'The King is dead! Long live the King!'

The Gordon Highlanders are seen marching up King Street after attending a parade at St Mary's church. The sight and sound of the battalion in all their regimental splendour was enough to attract a large crowd as the soldiers marched back to their barracks.

The 6th Battalion Gordon Highlanders are seen heading off from Bucksburn on August 6 1914 to take part in the First World War, and by 23 August the battalion had seen action against the Germans at the Battle of Mons. In 1917, Private Gordon McIntosh, a member of the battalion, was awarded the Victoria Cross when armed with a revolver and a single grenade, he waded across a stream under fire, working his way from shell hole to shell hole, killing a number of enemy gunners.

Aberdeen loves a procession, and none could be as grand as a parade to celebrate a new king. This was the scene in 1911 as a group on horseback, portraying Mary Queen of Scots, passed by the huge crowds in Union Street. George V was crowned King in 1910 and reigned until 1936.

Another scene from the same procession as it makes its way along Rosemount Viaduct towards His Majesty's Theatre. The costumes of the people on the float are quite elaborate and theatrical – it is a pity that the driver of the float is dressed in a suit and cap.

Aberdeen is perhaps fortunate that members of the Royal Family on their way to Balmoral can be persuaded to attend events taking place in the city. In 1925 the Duke of York attended the school sports day at Pittodrie Park. A keen sportsman, this future king, played at Wimbledon in the All-England tennis championship the following year.

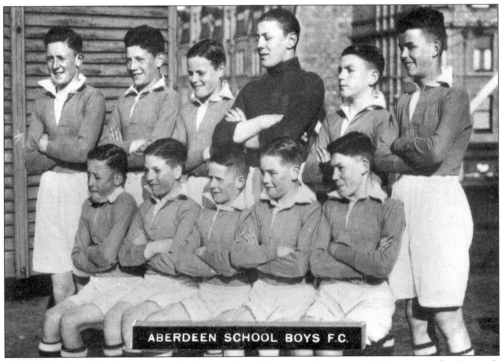

ABERDEEN SCHOOL BOYS F.C.

The Aberdeen schoolboy football team in the 1920s was a bit special. They won the Scottish Schools Cup on five occasions. They are from left to right, back row: J. Keay (Captain), J. Hendry, A. Burnett, T. Matthews, J. Park, J. Robertson. Front row: W. Hay, A. Davidson, J. Jappy, W. Kirton, J. Massie.

A group of future teachers and their tutors pose in front of the oldest part of Robert Gordons College (The Auld Hoose), built in 1732 for the education of poor boys. From 1912 part of the college was used as a training centre for teachers. Above the doorway, in the background, is a glimpse of the marble statue of Robert Gordon, carved by John Cheere.

Laying Memorial Stone, Unitarian Church, Aberdeen, 30/9/05

The Unitarian Church was founded in Aberdeen in 1833, and from 1840 held their services in premises in George Street. Under the leadership of the Rev. Alex Webster, a new church was built in Skene Street and Sir John Brunner MP was given the honour of officially laying the memorial stone at the ceremony in 1905. The Unitarian church and the Jehovah's Witnesses, to their mutual benefit, exchanged premises in 1989, a fine example of ecclesiastical cooperation. The Unitarian church today is based in Skene Terrace.

On the corner of Great Western Road and Cramford Road, a post office has been in business since 1906. In this 1917 picture the postmaster was G. J. A. Maclean, who remained in charge until he sold the business in 1931. How many stamps have been sold in all these years?

This photograph was taken in Menzies Road, Torry in 1922. The children are all well dressed with the exception of one boy who is barefooted. The only toys that were available consist of a metal hoop over the shoulder of one boy and a tin bath on the head of another boy, both to the right of the picture. In the background are two men in a horse and trap. The only names known from this group photograph are of a Johnny Gillespie and Bob Scott, but their location in the picture is unknown.